Notes on the Inner City

George Szirtes

Notes on the Inner City

20/20 **EYEWEAR**
PAMPHLET SERIES
2015

First published in 2015 by Eyewear Publishing Ltd
74 Leith Mansions, Grantully Road
London W9 1LJ United Kingdom

Typeset with graphic design by Edwin Smet
Printed in England by Lightning Source

ISBN 978-1-908998-73-6
WWW.EYEWEARPUBLISHING.COM

for Mauricio Montiel, 'El Hombre de Tweed'

Every thing possible to be believ'd is an image of truth —

William Blake Proverbs of Hell

Table of contents

1.

Nature is a pink elephant on stiletto heels.

The Minotaur carries his own ball of thread.

The early bird is a dead duck.

Two rats don't make a conversation.

Two goats don't make a choir.

Dogs don't talk to lampposts.

Wealth is a dog in a fur coat.

The dogs of war don't go to the dog show.

2.

The messenger arrives on a wooden horse.

The cause of peace often begins with the cutting out of tongues.

Politicians praise the cook but close the restaurant.

Argus in the corridors, Cyclops in the office.

The boss wears expensive blinkers.

3.

The general smiles: the crow whets its beak.

Heads are rolling, the mountain is moving.

If you chop the big tree it will bring down the little trees.

An iron glove fits any hand.

The weaker the man the bigger the fist.

The god of the first blow has many cousins.

Hot blood skates on thin ice.

Never mind the omelette, break the egg.

Bombs are tongues.

4.

Consistency is a lawn flattened to within an inch of its life.

The new official language of Pandemonium is in the pipeline as we speak.

Truths become lies when the wind is high.
I have morals. You have motives.
Indignation is a cheap suit off the market.
The table of high virtue is serving sweets again.
Wardrobe your grievances. They'll soon be back in fashion.
You can't have too many pointing fingers.
Always accuse the dead dog of stinking.
The ducking stool fits everyone.
Cinna's bad verses are reason enough.
Always recycle your victims.
The dead have turned in their graves long enough. Now it is our turn.
Bring back the king. We want to hang him again.
Extend your definitions: kill everyone.

5.
Raindrops are eyes without sockets.
In the land of the blind nobody can see a one-eyed man.
It is no easier finding two needles in a haystack.
A city of lost causes constantly needs to find new ones.
Don't beat about the bush. Burn the bush down.

6.
Summer in the flesh: winter in the bones.
This winter sunlight is for you.
The snow may like you but it will never love you.
The dead leaf understands the pavement.
End of the year: turn over a dead leaf.
Death makes cold calls.
May your fingernails survive you.

7.
Desire winds its own clock.
The teeth grapes; the palate wine; the skull champagne.
Beauty is uniform: the same sadness.
The wind is always speaking with its mouth full.

Under the skin, more skin. Under the heart, another heart.
There is no map to a dark room.
The stoppered heart, the smell of gas.
Always burn your bridges before building them.
I love you, says the cliff as the body falls.
Hard times miss soft landings.

8.
The mad will always find you at home.
The devil gets the best shoes.
The lost have no mouth but long nails.
The dead walk through small holes.
Death won't cure you.
The Furies have bright smiles.
The Kindly Ones don't mind waiting.

9.
Grace is all parentheses.
Laughter rots from the feet upwards.
The orchestra is in the brackets.
Leave your mouth open, the teeth fly out.
The cinemas of heaven show horror films at night.
Look for faces in the clouds till you find your own.
Everything would be all right in slow motion.
It is the even light that is the odd thing.

10.
Let us rationalise our orifices.
The soul smells of the body.
Those are not your fingers. Those are not your hands.
It is never too early to panic.

11.

Build your house of straws in the wind.
The wall with its ears, the mouth with its walls.
The officious live in small pockets.
It's hard to open the door with an elephant in the room.
The outcast may call himself what name he likes.

12.

Never understate the wound.
The high horse is the wounded horse.
The high horse sees no fences.
Keep a spare civil tongue in your head.

13.

He used to be a statue.
His brakes have no brakes.
All glove, no hand.
Wolf in the street, sheep in the house.
He was a kind man according to the crows.
Honest enough to tell a bare faced lie.

15.

A fox in gloves is not necessarily a flower.
Who will see the fox in a fire?
A fox is fire without smoke.
A fox in a yard is a circumscribed fox.

16.

Too many pins, not enough angels.
Babel is the only hotel in town.
The mirrors in Babel are all broken.

17.

The flying carpet is the one you get rolled up in.

Every dog has his favourite lamppost.

Never disturb a grandmother when she is sucking an egg.

18.

Pleading innocence is the lowest form of wit.

Every meteorite has got your name on it.

A hollow tube will play what the wind tells it to.

Tight purse keeps loose change.

The last moment has the deepest pockets.

The more kindness by commission, the more cruelty by omission.

19.

The smaller the dog the bigger the eyes.

Let the fish run the fish stall.

A land without a gun is like a snake without a tongue.

Shoot your teachers just in case.

20.

The books are coming home to roost.

A clear sky is considering clouds.

Grass talking, trouble brewing.

The blank sheet lies.

It was a woman's face deep in the sea, self-constructed, as if one could make the moon out of flesh, bone, colour, reflection.

There was nothing there to touch. The sea was warm, the face gazed through it in its act of self-construction which involved gazing.

This was it. The muse-face. The construction. The self-made moon on its seabed. The astonishing in its perpetual process of construction.

This was the face that could give and consume, made out of myth and moonlight, making itself, turning itself into gaze.

And I have seen her, said the words. That gaze constructs itself as the compulsive act. And a cold shiver ran down him. And more words.

Make me a poet, said the words of the poem. Undermine me, said the gaze. Be discontent, said the muse. For ever, said the moon in the words.

These are old tropes, said the muse. But you must keep opening them. The poem lies beyond the opening, at the origin of words.

But muse, said the poem, if I am not the construction I desire to be I will die. Be sceptical, said the muse. Believe, said the poem.

Eyes

Those heavy eyes. We took them out and plugged them into the mains for a recharge. They kept blinking then settled into a steady gaze.

We took the eyes and slipped them into our pockets. Let them see darkness visible. Let them count the bills, let them register the account.

Maintaining eyes is not easy. You have to encourage them, gain their confidence, call them some name or other. Let them look through you.

One day the eyes flew off. Not very far, just to the back of the yard. They had never seen the world, nor was this it. It was a yard. An eye.

We found life deep in them. The eyes spoke to us, whispering something grey-green, as if they were pure sweet water. They drank us down.

We knew the eyes were the only thing that mattered. They knew it. We were what they drank, what ours consumed. Eyes were vitally important.

Look thy last, they said. It was a courtyard in the city. There were graffiti. The walls were made to be looked at. We kept looking.

We were fabulously wealthy. We rode horses in our sleep. Our walls dripped art. We knew everything & nothing. It was ours to lose.

We were in heaven in a smart car. The streets saluted us as we passed. Behind us, like a honeymoon trail of trash, the big stores, grinning.

Our servants were invisible. They ran about with heavy trunks containing their own lives. When we tipped them they glowed like embers.

Sometimes we wanted rain. We knew the right people. They'd come running with their dry excuses. It was the excuses that we really wanted.

For all our wealth we were unhappy. The sex was bad but the service was excellent. Our salt cellars were pure gold but our feet were tin.

We dispensed largesse between meals. Crowds came to our funeral. They were sporting buttonholes of dead flowers. We fed them caviare.

Our dreams of avarice were spectacular affairs. Mountains moved. We had a fleet of empty cars. The music under the streets was perfect.

Shari found herself in India. Martin was in China. We were in several places at once at the centre of the earth. We paid and left.

We had people to do things for us. We paid them fortunes. When we woke we were those people. We led full and interesting lives on hard cash.

Off with his head, screamed the queen. And his. And his. And that other one's. I don't trust heads. I don't like your nose.

The boy at the queen's side took out his catapult and shot the man's nose off. It was his first act in the dynasty.

The space where the man's nose had been was a vacancy that should have been filled. A man without a nose is an offence, said the queen.

The queen died. The noseless man's head was impaled on a spike. All was well in the kingdom now the boy was on the throne.

The ghost of the noseless man hovered around the palace corridors. The boy-king had it arrested for nothing less than treason.

The generals of the army all had noses but some noses were bigger than others. A degree of consistency was required.

All the generals were sheared of their noses by royal order. Their faces were an offence to the boy-king. He sheared them of their heads.

More ghosts crowded the palace. The boy-king had them arrested. His catapult became the state emblem, vert on gules.

The people are hungry, reported the cowering messenger. The boy-prince sheared off his nose then his head. Feed them to the people, he said.

The people rose against the boy-king. He had them arrested and decapitated. My people are ghosts, he said to no-one in particular.

The Politics of Wind

'To see the wind, with a man his eyes, it is unpossible, the nature of it is so fine, and subtle, yet this experience of the wind had I once myself' – Roger Ascham, *Toxophilus*

No one has seen the wind, only its effects. But what about the effect on the eyes, how they close against it, how they seem to be seeing it?

When leaves raise hands it is not because they want to leave the room. They might want to get in. Or they are simply helpless, saying: stop!

The reality that is the wind meets the reality that is the glass. They don't cancel each other out, they stand there looking at each other.

The wind will blow us away! It eats the revolution's children. It proposes another revolution, and another. It is the politics of gust.

The wind is inside our arms and legs. It shudders through ribs and vertebrae. It has its own body but it wants ours, both heart and mind.

Now then Herr Schmidt, that tie does not become you. You shirt is unfitting to your station, nor is that a real dog.

After all the half-baked imitations a real dog was welcome in the house which had been empty far too long.

The real dog was on its way home from work. In the darkness spectral dogs were watching patiently as the bus approached.

The real dog lay by the fire. The spectral dogs were preparing to enter it.

It was lonely being a real dog. One had teeth of one's own to look after. One's tongue tended to curl itself in and out of one's mouth.

One may be granted doghood, but that is not the same as being granted reality. One needs a real tongue. Like this, he growled.

Was there just the one real dog? Was that too much of a burden? The real dog was caught between two stools. Nor were the stools real.

How to distinguish oneself from fake dogs of the imagination? How to carry oneself, to have a certain port in air? Only a real dog would do.

One counts one's feet. There really are four of them. That would not have been the case had one not been a real dog. Or most likely not.

The responsibility of being a real dog. The honour of being a real dog. The acuity of one's hearing. One's nose. These were not nothing.

The real dog buttoned his waistcoat and took himself off the leash. Go, little dog, he whispered, enter the book, run free.

1

When he lay NE-SW his mother's ghost appeared in the jar.

2

When he sat by the east-facing window there was only the cat looking at the table.

3

When he walked by the church little devils were ringing bells over the field and a dead thrush lay on the path.

4

When he walked by the river a woman with three dogs asked him a question he couldn't answer.

5

When he felt in his pocket he discovered his father's old purse, soft, leather with a modicum of stateless small change.

6

When the radio was on it was as if his ears were not his own. They belonged to someone in another world.

7

When he sat in the armchair the rain was describing an event he couldn't remember.

8

While he was waiting at the bus stop his own mortality passed him in a car and waved to him.

9

When he walked through the door the air was waiting for him with a faint smile on its face and a key in its hand.

10

When he looked in the mirror he was relieved to find himself, only better and somehow more complete. He resolved to return there more often.

He talked of God at times. He scribbled furious notes to Him. The picture of an old man with a long white beard hung upside down in the hall.

Several times he had survived by the skin of his teeth. By now he was wearing dentures. His luck was bound to run out.

There was a dispute about land. He planted a flag in the middle of a field. The wind blew it away. No more flags, he declared.

His brown suit was creased, his grey suit was torn. He had patches on his elbows. His eyes looked all ways at once. Where am I, he asked.

I am the father you never had, he told me. If you see me on the stairs tip your hat, should you be wearing one, or at least comb your hair.

One can have too many fathers, he told me. People are foolish. I was never yours but you are free to invent me. Just ask permission first.

There was something paw-like about his hands. Fur gathered at his wrist and up his arms. I may be simian, he said, but I'm all you've got.

Your mother was an angel to me, he said. She was ethereal at night and fully winged by day. Her laugh was like rust on an old fork.

You may not think much of me, said the father I never had, but I am not entirely an absence. I have teeth. At least I did once.

The phone call is dead said the article – and it had gone dead. The voice in the head traveling, unmapped, on its own long trip wire.

And then the phone went dead. It was the death of the vertical, the death of the coil, the death of the body on its table of grave-clothes.

And then the phone went dead. The closed mouth, the unstopped ear. The panic of finger & throat, from shrill bell to dull hum. It's for you.

And then the phone went dead & graves began to ring with their urgent demands. They threatened, they cajoled, fluttered shrouds at the sky.

And then the phone went dead and centuries of dense silence shook, tipping over into the alternative universe of birdcall, rainfall, hail.

*

The slender body of the phone. The voluptuousness of its windings. Its insistence on being heard, the hand still warm from holding it.

We were waiting for you to ring. Bell within waiting for bell without. The mutual ringing. The mute earthquake of the flesh. The ear hot.

It rang and rang and no-one answered because it was not to be seen anywhere and might not be where you expected the ringing to appear.

When we last spoke the voices were elsewhere, in boxes, in hallways, in restaurants and bars, in our heads, even then exiting, ringing off.

You had to be there, not here or just anywhere, there where the instrument was located, pinned like an insect, chirring, unable to move.

They were writing Valentines to each other when the words began to splinter. They are more beautiful like that, they thought. Tiny and clear.

He drew a word from his pocket. It was old and yellowed. Give it to me, she said. I'll wear it when it occurs to me to do so. Maybe tomorrow.

So he bought her a dress of words and she put them on. Now try dancing, he said. You spell them out first, she said.

See this word 'love' he said. You can have it. I have more back home, but none as nice as this. Try it. It was hotter than she had expected.

She held the word at arm's length. She had the most beautiful arms. The word was not important. It was the arms. The hands. The fingers.

The word 'sex' was never mentioned. It stood outside the door looking at its shoes so she came out and polished them.

I am sure it was in my handbag, she said. Then he drew it out from behind her ear. It sounded like the word but it was only a close rhyme.

What is the right word for your body, she asked. I couldn't possibly pronounce it, he replied. But I have written it down.

There is a word in my mouth, she said. Open, he said. Yes, I think I can see it. Breathe gently. It's one of mine. Now blow.

She put the word down by his hand. He picked it up and examined it. It was breathing. It had a scent. He popped it into his mouth.

This does not make sense, she wrote. What she wrote was clear, precise, legible. It did not make sense. The clearer it got, the less sense it made.

Nothing makes sense. The moon leaking light, the wind prising open the window. She wrote leaning forward; her writing cursive, sealed, clean.

To construct a shelter out of the impossible, she wrote, one needs perfection. This is not it. This is not a shelter. It is writing.

If only the act of writing were self-completing, she wrote as the moth in the window fluttered and rattled. This is neither moth nor window.

If only yearning could be written, she wrote. Something in the distance suggested completion. She wrote towards it as clearly as she could.

Every time I begin a sentence I can feel its end approaching. Once it arrives, I can stop, she wrote and placed a neat period at 'stop'.

There is nothing to be gained, she wrote. The desk light threw a shadow that suggested something else. The sentence was moving towards it.

I am writing, she wrote. I am writing this. What she wrote was the shadow on the desk. This was what she had written. It had a shape.

It might have been a letter. It could have been an observation. She wrote it with the possibility of either. It was the cold page shivering.

Was there another to write to or was it merely talking to oneself? She read the thought again. Now she was someone else. She would reply.

Whatever I write is a requirement, she wrote. It has to be written into existence. I am writing it. It is here not elsewhere, yet beyond me.

If I write myself into exhaustion there will be only night, dawn, and a full page of writing. Her writing was neat, without flourishes.

So she laid down her pen. It made a shadow on the paper. There was the exclamation mark she never used. It appeared: the shape of never.

The noises outside were inchoate. They were seeping into the room like a stain she had to write.

One writes the stain noise makes, she wrote. Stain is the noise under the word that spreads across the paper. I am writing it as best I can.

One always wants the impossible, she wrote. This too is impossible but at least I am writing it. Or something else that is impossible.

The wind outside had to be written. She wrote it inside, on a sheet of paper, on a desk. The wind remained outside but now it made sense.

She picked the sheet of paper off the floor where the draught had blown it. Her writing was still there on the paper. It had not vanished.

She picked herself up from the floor where the sheet had landed. I am still here, she noted. I am not the wind. I am not nothing. Here I am.

I am writing sense into the world, she wrote somewhat grandiosely, then crossed out the last four words. Now it made sense.

1

What she told herself was true, she thought, and wondered what else she could tell herself.

I have invented fictions of myself that seem truer than what I think I know, she thought.

The fiction of self as invention is the only credible fiction, she thought.

Half my face is invented on a groundwork of fact, she thought.

I have found a new face for myself, she thought.

2

My body too is an invention but it's the only body I know. The trouble is it makes itself up as it goes along without me.

She had made an attempt to invent a language of unsourced gestures. How to say yes without looking as though one did. How not to lie.

Invention is not lying. When we invent ourselves we are discovering truth, she said, smiling at something in the mirror.

Inventing is a way of happening. It's a song I thought I remembered that I was making up. It sounds like this, she sang.

If I could ungender myself, she thought, I would think differently. My very face would have a different value, especially to myself.

3

So she invented him and equipped him with certain faults that she then attempted to correct. Then she had to reinvent the faults.

This is your nature, she said to him. I should know. I invented you. But she had forgotten something. Now she had to invent that too.

What she invented was a man prepared to invent her in return. This seemed only fair.

I never believe a thing he says, she said to herself. He is a fiction in the interim. He is an anecdote no one believes.

I am using an invented female self to reflect on my degendered manhood, she admitted to herself.

Under the eyelids real eyes invented themselves. The conceptual eyes of a real world. Invention is gorgeous, she wrote.

4

Here was the third voice, the one not used to speaking itself, only others. It had a foot in either gender. It had washed and shaved.

It was night in the imagined city. It could stay that way unless she invented morning, and it was her prerogative to do so.

The body is invention, said the blood. This organ is not a figment of my imagination but this genuinely mortal voice is.

I am tired, said the voice. I must invent more energy for myself. She was wearing a stunning pair of shoes. She must live up to them.

This fictive voice knows more than I do. This bare floor is something I tread with my invented feet. She wept and moved forward.

5

And so she unwrote herself from the fictions that defined her. Here was night. The street was real. All the lights were on.

1

I am nowhere, she thought, checking her bearings. Here was here. There was there. It was the rest that was the problem.

2

Finding oneself here is not enough, she thought. There seemed to be a conversation going on in the distance but it might have been thunder.

3

We define ourselves by whatever lies close to hand, she thought. But nothing seemed to be close, only the sound of approaching thunder.

4

The real question is whether the thunder that sounds like conversation is threatening, she thought, and whether it is likely to arrive.

5

Arriving was the problem. Anticipation was natural. Being here was natural. She was nowhere in particular. Nothing could arrive.

6

We can't tell conversation from thunder, she concluded. Things approach us without declaring themselves, without definition.

7

Would you mind if I asked you how close you are, she asked the thunder, which was only a growling that might have been a conversation.

8

Conversation is more like rain than thunder, she thought. It is not raining. Not here at least. I am doing all the talking.

9

The true problem is isolation, she thought. It is being here, exactly where I am, with the conversation elsewhere. And it's raining.

10

She felt the rain on her skin. It was talking to her. There was thunder in her ears. This is conversation, she thought. I am talking.

Symbol

A country dog flits across the street;

The old paper mills! The green pure water. – Sarah Kirsch, tr Anne Stokes

She awoke upside down in a moment of quiet. This would do. No need to say anything. It was only when her breasts were ablaze she noticed she had become a symbol of something. Now to find out what. She was composing herself as one had to in order to know who one was, assembling the pieces with a particularly pleasing fury. How far am I symbol, she wondered. How far not?

Was it enriching or reductive to be a symbol? Is a golden body more valuable than one of flesh and blood? Was blood a symbol? If she turned slightly she could see herself over her shoulder in the mirror. There was the symbol, in the flesh, through glass. Seeing myself is being outside myself, she said. The seen me is out there perceiving the real me as a symbol, as distance, as siren. (Far away a symbol was waiting and watching, as symbols do.)

He was writing her. I was writing him. I was being written and read by her at a symbolic, faintly erotic distance where nothing would happen. So they lived happily after, someone was writing. Someone had to, after all, preferably someone anonymous, she thought. Someone like us. Can't we all just try to be nice to each other, asked the anonymous voice. That's the way the anonymous voice tends to talk, she thought.

And so she turned to look through the window where three symbolic statues stood in a symbolic garden that needed attention. Nature is a forest of symbols, the symbolist had written. Nature is naked, wrote the naturist. The imagination needs clothes, she suggested.

1.

She began with the rope and the ice cube but then the bell rang and the traffic stopped.

2.

Once upon a time at a very precise address the king was filing his teeth. There was war in the land and it was cold.

3.

The storyteller paused. There were certain facts beyond facts and the narrative was less absurd than it should have been.

4.

It was everything then. Then it was not, or only partly. The graphs showed it. Under the graphs, the snow. Under the snow, amnesia.

5.

Tell me a joke, said one. That is not a joke, they said. The joke shrugged. It had been here before.

6.

What is the point of language, they complained. It was always the wrong language, especially for posing questions in. There must be another.

7.

The sedge had withered from the lake and yet a bird was singing. The knight-at-arms turned around. There were plenty of dames in the sea.

8.

Once upon a time there was a context without an event. All around it a tumult of events. The problem of nothing happening.

9.

Pass me the knife, she said. Her voice was like frost on the brambles. I will not abide snow, she declared and turned off the light.

10.

The sheer romance of it! They arranged the vocables into mythical narratives. How they shone! What lives they led! Language was gold!

They were silent as they packed the truck. They had arranged first-class travel but now they were lost for words. Trunk, idiots! Trunk!

The wind was lost down an alleyway. The maps were never adequate. You just blew into town and were expected to know.

I never signed for this, the mouse complained to the cat. Small print, said the cat. The dead have no word for tort, said the cat's lawyer.

If we spread our fingers, she said, the life-force has more wriggle-room. But it didn't. It just lay there like a stone herring.

Plague was raging through the town. Parochialism is the curse of modernity, remarked a theorist. Besides, I'm hungry.

You're under arrest, said the cop. The deckchairs stared defiantly back at him. They'd been here before. They knew their rights.

In a distant land the forces of darkness were gathering. Where are we going, asked one. Here's the brochure, said another. Can't you read?

It was Newcastle and 3am. It could have been worse. There were, after all, the shrews and the voles. Not tonight. No, thank you.

Let me put it to you that your eyes were closed and that you never saw the incident in which my client allegedly put out your eyes.

Surely there couldn't be life there, they thought as they cruised past Earth. Where was the courtesy, the bonhomie, where the cute symbols?

There was no one in the street. There was no one in the house. Where were they? Where was the car? What had happened to the plot?

The plot was beside the point. The point was to remain plotless. He opened a box left behind from the last plot. Nothing there.

An empty box was no clue. He checked his notebook. It was brand new. He took his pen and wrote a few random words that might mean something.

The street was indecipherable. That much was clear. But was it pointless to think so? That was what the words said. He wrote more words.

The mystery of the empty street was no less mysterious than the empty house. No car appeared though it was what the plot required.

He thought back to the time he had spent by the sea. There had been gulls and pebbles. Such things had a point and might add up to a plot.

The instruments had been well hidden. That is if they were instruments. He took a key from his pocket. All he needed now was a door.

The sea was at the door but the door was elsewhere. He wrote more words. He imagined a door. There was the smell of the sea to consider.

Somewhere in the attic lay the clue to the whereabouts of the house. Once he had located the house he was sure to find the sea.

Was there any point in having a key if there were no door? That remained to be discovered. Life is plotless, he decided. He must invent one.

You can't invent everything. You could invent a sea and imagine a house with a door. You could open that door. You could smell the sea.

Whatever had happened had stopped happening. Something else was happening but what was it? What had the sea to do with it? Or the key?

This seemed to be the plot. It was as close to a plot as he could find. He wrote the plot down. He imagined the door. He turned the key.

The empty house and the empty street remained empty. The car must be elsewhere. The corpse would be in it, assuming there was a corpse.

There had to be a corpse. The plot demanded it. It was pointless without a corpse. He would have to invent one. But there was no car.

You could invent the car with the corpse in it. You could invent a sea at a door. You could open the door with the key. If it fitted.

You could invent moonlight. You could invent a lamp post. You could invent an alley, a corpse, and a car. You could invent a point.

The smell of the sea remained. That did not have to be invented. He wrote the words 'the sea' in his notebook. The sea was the point.

The point was the crime of which the corpse was the result. The corpse was in the car that remained to be invented. The sea was real enough.

The sea at least was real. It always had been. His notebook said so. The door must be nearby. He had the key. He was master of the situation.

This story was found in a Christmas cracker two years ago. It had an excellent punchline. That's why it is here now.

This story is a quotation from another story but it was not plagiarised. However, with some luck, it might be.

This story is short and to the point. He was born. A terrible thing happened. The story is going to end right here. Now it has ended.

This is a 'post-modern' story. Note the inverted commas. It is self-aware. It may even be post-post-modern. But then again it might not.

This story about a raccoon involves an early twentieth-century dinner-set. There is absolutely no reason why it should not.

This story has a sensational angle. It is currently looking for it. Once it has found it it will no longer be interested in it.

This story is nothing but rain. It begins in rain and ends in rain. I suppose that is a spoiler. I shouldn't have mentioned the rain.

This story is going to change the world. In fact it already has. It feels no need to prove that fact, it is after all just a story.

This story has two mice crawling through it. The two mice walk into a bar. They order a drink. Every story has a point. This is it.

This story is a variant on one you have already read. If you haven't read it before it will make no sense to you. That's what literature is.

This story is probably pornographic but who knows nowadays. It's all subjective, isn't it? There! You just missed it. Feel free to rewind.

This story is waiting for publication. Wait a moment. This is publication. Buy here or order from Amazon. See reviews.

This story is by an absolute master of such stories. Note the flow of the sentence from capital letter to the final perfectly placed period.

This story is one my grandmother told me as she was falling down the chimney after a collision with an owl. It's that kind of story.

This story is a literary landmark, recognised as such by the leading critics of the time. That was then of course. Today it's up for grabs.

This story is translated from the original by a machine designed for the purpose. You can talk to it and it will not disappoint you.

This story is not that story. I should make that clear before we start or else that story might be confused with this one.

This story originated in a joke told by a Peruvian architect at a bus stop in Lima. Its local flavour may be lost on some but do persist!

This stroy is fllu of topys. The cypo etodir is on hiolady. The plubshier alopogises for any aganrams taht are nto toyps.

This story is minimalist. That was and continues to be its project. Any sentence after the first is to be regarded as a footnote.

What he did and what he was were merging into what he was perceived to be, or what he perceived others as perceiving him to be.

The first person plural was walking down the street directly towards him. I can't be there too, he thought. But he was.

I could never be Them, he thought. Though I could be Him. Or Her. But not while they're Them. His grammar was coming to pieces in his mouth.

Could he himself be The Other. Was he out there somewhere hiding behind a bush waiting to pop out and cry: So there you are!

He blinked. Sometimes there is no alternative to blinking. The world is still there but at least it has been blinked at.

Does world blink back, he wondered. Surely that couldn't be the world winking at him. Hello world. Hello sailor.

Hurrah for The World! It would be on later, top of the bill. You waited hours for it but that was the point. It would appear.

The World was on stage and looking directly at him, no mistake about it. And it winked. Hello sailor, it winked. Hello sailor. Hello.

There was a corpse-self he preferred not to think about. And why should he? He was only ninety-eight and still in foul health

He looked into his own eyes and straight through them, the gaze emerging from the back of his skull through two clean holes.

EYEWEAR PUBLISHING

BEN STAINTON EDIBLES

MEL PRYOR DRAWN ON WATER

MICHAEL BROWN UNDERSONG

MATT HOWARD THE ORGAN BOX

RACHAEL M NICHOLAS SOMEWHERE NEAR IN THE DARK

BETH TICHBORNE HUNGRY FOR AIR

GALE BURNS OPAL EYE

PIOTR FLORCZYK BAREFOOT

LEILANIE STEWART A MODEL ARCHAEOLOGIST

SHELLEY ROCHE-JACQUES RIPENING DARK

SAMANTHA JACKSON SMALL CRIES

V.A. SOLA SMITH ALMOST KID

GEORGE SZIRTES NOTES ON THE INNER CITY

JACK LITTLE ELSEWHERE

DAMILOLA ODELOLA LOST & FOUND

KEITH JARRETT I SPEAK HOME

www.ingramcontent.com/pod-product-compliance
Ingram Content Group UK Ltd.
Pitfield, Milton Keynes, MK11 3LW, UK
UKHW021316090726
13667UKWH00007B/51